Perfectly Normal Autistic

Michelle Swan

Books in the "Living Autistically" series:

Fierce Autistic Heart   (2024)
Authentic Autistic Living   (2024)
Perfectly Normal Autistic   (2024)

Original cover art by Emory Thorsen.

ISBN 978-0-6488711-6-3 (print - paperback)
ISBN 978-0-6488711-8-7 (EPUB)
ISBN 978-0-9756585-2-9 (PDF)

Published in Australia by Michelle Swan
© Michelle Swan 2024
This work is copyright. Apart from any use permitted under the Copyright Act 1968, no part may be reproduced by any process, nor may any other exclusive right be exercised, without the permission of the author.
contact@hellomichelleswan.com

This book is for informational purposes only. It does not constitute advice, and should not be used as replacement for professional support and/or diagnosis.

This book is dedicated to Mark
who taught me things about life and myself that
I wouldn't have learned without him.
And because my life is better
from having known him.

contents

introduction	i
empathy	1
masking	10
labour	14
inertia	21
rigidity	25
independent	31
interdependent	34
pendulum	39
labels	44
paradox	49
strong	52
functioning	55
uninspirational	60
noncompliant	69
assertive	72
normal	77
courageous	81
perfect	85

introduction

"Perfectly Normal Autistic" is the third in my Living Autistically series of books of short essays on my experience of realising that I am Autistic and finding ways to move toward self understanding and self acceptance so I can live my life well. To just be me in the ways I need to in order to reduce the pain, discomfort, and difficulty I was experiencing before I knew I am Autistic.

A key part of this process was realising that I am not a broken normal person, but rather a normal autistic person. I had to realise this in order to give myself permission to be who I actually am instead of trying to be someone I'm not and can't be.

It might sound obvious. But it wasn't. And it wasn't easy to do. I haven't finished learning it yet, and I never will …. Growth and healing are ongoing tasks.

As with the first two books, each chapter can be read as a stand alone piece, and there is no need to read this book in order. In this series of books, I'm not sharing with you to try to solve all your challenges. The information in the books is intended to be an introduction to ideas that will help you start to understand yourself and how you might proceed to creating a better life. Each chapter talks about a quality, characteristic, or concept that has been important to me along my way to creating a life that suits me and my needs well. Maybe some of them will be things you need to consider too.

My best wishes to you all as you find your own way to be.

Michelle

empathy

I've thought a lot about empathy and the common perception that autistic people lack it. Thankfully this perception is held less strongly than it used to be, but it persists to some extent. Societally, we understand empathy in very simplistic ways, and I think sometimes misunderstand it. I'm sure this contributes to the idea that autistic people lack empathy.

My experience with feeling empathy is that I know I feel it, in fact I feel other peoples emotional experience quite strongly. All humans experience co-regulation of nervous systems to some extent, and my ability to sense other peoples upset, anger, happiness, fear, and excitement seems to be greater than a lot of people I know. However, other peoples communications about how they are feeling and what they are thinking are often confusing.

In my efforts to understand why I experience confusion in relation to other people emotions and moods, I have done a fair bit of reading. I was really interested to learn that there is more than one type of empathy! I now think of empathy as having three types, or parts.

Affective empathy, or emotional empathy, is when we can sense that other people are feeling something. We may not have experienced the stimulus for the emotion, but we can share in its experience with the other person as though the emotion is contagious because our nervous systems co-regulate.

Cognitive empathy, or perspective taking, is the ability to understand someone else's experience from a rational and logical viewpoint. This is a skill that requires us to be able to accept that the other persons experience is valid and real to them, even if we don't think we would experience the situation in the same way.

Compassionate empathy, or what we often call sympathy, is being moved to help the person in some way to manage the situation and/or their experience of it.

Sympathy doesn't require us to have affective or cognitive empathy, we can be motivated to try to be helpful without those foundations, however without them our attempts to help will quite likely be perceived as insensitive. This is often what causes an accusation of a lack of empathy.

My observation of most autistic people is that they have plenty of affective empathy, even to the point of being hyper empathetic - experiencing other peoples emotions so strongly that it can be overwhelming and result in a lack of demonstrative compassionate empathy.

Another observation I have made of most autistic people is that they seem to struggle with cognitive empathy. I think that because autistic experience is so different than non autistic experience, figuring out the logical reason for the other persons emotions can be quite a challenge. And I don't think this is a one way challenge- non autistic people have difficulty with cognitive empathy toward autistic people too.

To personalise these observations, and give an example of how autistic people experience empathy, I've included some of my own thoughts and logical processes of trying to understand others, transcribed from some journaling I did.

> People say they are ok, but I can be almost positive they aren't because I can feel that they aren't.... But because they say they are okay I doubt myself and feel confused – how can I be so wrong so often?.... then later I find out they weren't ok, so I wonder why they lied. Then I realise I lie too, because deep down I know the rules say you can't be yourself and its not safe to leave yourself exposed and vulnerable.
>
> Maybe we aren't close enough friends for them to trust me with their pain. I understand that. But I still feel the pain. It moves through the space between us and rests in my lap.
>
> Maybe we are close but there is another reason they don't want to share with me right now. I understand that too, because sometimes I don't have words, or energy, or resilience enough to strip myself naked emotionally, in front of anyone, not even someone I know and trust. But I still ache

with them, their pain sitting on my shoulders like a boulder. I feel it like it is my own.

It's hard to explain. I don't know why I can't turn off this sense I have of all the emotions around me. I guess it's similar to the way I hear every sound. The noises and the feelings just somehow reach through into my brain. They are loud and intrusive and I can't ignore them. Both are more intense if I am already anxious in my own right. But even if I am not they creep through no matter how hard I might try to ignore them. Through into my consciousness demanding my attention. Distracting me from things I should be doing. Forcing me into overwhelm. Necessitating the start of another deliberate withdrawal for self care.

I try to be responsible for my own feelings- to learn to separate others feelings from mine and not carry them with me even though I cannot help but feel them. I know that is up to me and not them. I can't expect others to not feel their feelings, I can't expect them to care for my feelings when they are struggling, I can't expect that everyone in the world will feel safe to confide in me when they are having a hard time. It really is on me to manage my own sensitivity to emotions, this hyper-empathy that causes me pain and overwhelm.

….. yet I cannot help but wonder if the world wouldn't be easier, and maybe even safer, if we all spoke the truth. When I know someone is sad or hurt or upset or distressed, "I'm fine" makes no sense at all. We lie and say we are ok because we don't want to share….. but why don't we speak the truth instead?

"How are you?"
"Not great…. but I'll be ok, I don't need to talk about it"

"Are you alright?"
"No I'm not, but I don't have the energy to talk about it right now"

"What's wrong?"
"I'm having a hard time. Thanks for checking, but I've got the support I need to get through it, I don't need to talk right now."

"You seem upset… can I help?"
"I am upset…. but I can't discuss it at the moment. Could you check on me in a day or two, I'd love a listening ear by then when I've had some time to think things through a bit."

These answers I can understand. They make sense. I am comfortable with knowing you are struggling when you confirm it for me and let me know what you need or don't need from me.

As much as I feel all the things others feel and I find that overwhelming, it is so much harder knowing something is wrong but having that denied and the knowledge left hanging there with no way to process it. I think people don't want to bother me with their feelings so they decide to hide them from me, but I already feel them.

I worry that others don't tell me and that means maybe they don't tell anyone. I worry that they are not ok and that they are unsupported, alone and isolated. I hate to feel isolated and disconnected so I think others must too.

Regardless of who is empathetic and who isn't, open communication would help us all, I think.

I believe that feelings, in all their intensity are a gift, not a burden …. yet I am still learning how to appreciate hyper-empathy in myself. The process of trying to manage the impact of my feelings and other peoples all at the same time is difficult. I see it as invaluable and so I persist with it, but it is still difficult.

I believe that acknowledging that many autistic people are hyper-empathetic, without judging that as a bad thing but rather deciding to make some adjustments to the way we communicate in light of that understanding, would also be helpful to us all.

As I reflected on this journalling, I can see where I have the ability to know what others are feeling (affective empathy), and a strong desire to help (compassionate empathy, or sympathy), but struggle with understanding why they are experiencing what they are (cognitive empathy), which impacts on my ability to demonstrate my care (sympathy that can be recognised by others).

I think this is the case for a lot of autistic and otherwise neurodivergent people. Surely the remedy to the misunderstandings that we call lack of empathy is to be curious and communicate directly about our experiences and needs?

masking

I am autistic. Everything about me is autistic. I do everything I do autistically. Over my nearly 50 years I have learned, often quite deliberately, to do things in ways that you will interpret as "normal". But, I am still autistic, even when you can't tell I am by watching my behaviour. I am using a strategy called masking to blend in. I am passing as non-autistic.

The masking that I do is for your comfort and for mine.

It is for your comfort, in that when I seem to be "normal" you aren't scared of me, you don't feel a need to find explanations for my behaviour, and you don't feel a need to go out of your way to support me in anyway, or to have to do things to help me that you might find inconvenient.

It is for my comfort, in that when I do not inconvenience you, you treat me better- you speak to me kindly, you value my words more, you respect me. When you don't know that I am autistic. You also expect more from me. You assume I am capable. I hear your conversations and comments in schools, sport clubs, and community settings. I am aware of you talking to each other about the "special" people. I know you have different expectations for us. I hear your jokes about Rainman and Sheldon. I see you keep seperate awards for the disabled. I notice you look sideways at the people you see as different from you.

So I have figured out how to be accepted by you. It is by not being myself when I am around you.

But it is a double edged sword. Because I am not the same as you. I am autistic. So even though I might be able to make myself appear to be like you for a while in most situations and contexts, there are some things I just cannot do, and some I can only do up to a certain point before my resources are stretched beyond capacity and I can't mask my autisticness any longer. I know what the social expectation is. I just can't always meet it. I feel upset about it. Embarrassed. Ashamed.

My internal self talk mimics your outward expressions, "you can do better", "pull it together", "come on Michelle, try harder". Just like the knowledge that people want me to be a certain way, I take it on and internalise it. In the same way that almost everyone around me unintentionally taught me as a child that conformity is the goal, I reinforce to myself that I need to be what you expect.

And I push myself closer and closer to a meltdown or a shutdown, for your comfort. I do my best to hide away from you during these times. I stay home, in my bed, and I "rest".

Sometimes, though, I push myself so hard that I get to a point where I can't mask any longer, and I am not home yet, and you will see.

My behaviour will change from what you have come to expect from me. You will call me "angry", "clumsy", "antisocial", "rude", "awkward", "aggressive", or "weird". If you bring it up with me I will sometimes just say "I am tired". But I am simply being autistic in public. In a child it might look like a tantrum. In an autistic adult it often looks like a sudden withdrawal with no explanation. It often looks like unexplained tears that you assume are unjustified because you don't see the reason for them. You might call them weakness. They are not. They are a sign of strength and determination. And even the tears are for your comfort. They are what happens when I know I have to shut down for my own health and safety, but I choose not to in order to do something you expect of me.

And later, when I am alone, I feel intense anger. At myself. For choosing you, again, over my own self care. Because my masking isn't honest and it lacks integrity. It hides who I am. The benefit for me is short lived and fraught with complications. There is nothing wrong with me. Nor any real reason why I should change myself to conform with your standards of normality. It is a burden that I carry for you. And I wish I wouldn't do it.

labour

Sometimes I have significant difficulty managing the often perceived to be small things of a normal life. Cleaning, shopping, planning meals, answering emails. I learned about executive function fairly soon after realising I am Autistic. Some days I have little trouble getting through the things I need and want to do, other days I have trouble getting anything started, and other days can be anything in between. For a long time though, I had no success in reliably identifying what the specific triggers for increased impairment in my executive function was.

Things that I had identified as having an impact on my executive function included: sustained loud noise, unexpected short loud noise, bright light, flashing light, being touched a lot within a period of time, size of a task, tiredness, illness, unusually busy days and weeks, unexpected change, changes that cause me to alter my routines, anticipation of change, being in a large group of people, needing to process a large amount of communication done by speaking and listening, text walls, and more.

But while I realised that all of the above can be things that affect my executive function, I also know that when these things affect me more than usual it is a sign my executive function is already impaired. I cannot satisfactorily say these things are a cause of executive function impairment when they are also something I recognise as being more of a problem when my executive function is already impaired. Or, to say it "academically", I am not confident that these things are present purely due to causation, because I see evidence of a correlational relationship. Because of this I was still been looking for a root cause of my executive function impairments.

Then I learned about the concept of emotional labour.

As I was first reading on it I felt that the idea of emotional labour was new to me. But over time I realised that I knew about it, I just didn't know that I knew it. You see, for a very long time I understood about myself that being around people drains to me to the point of needing time doing literally nothing, even though I want company and connection. I just hadn't realised it was the emotional, empathic part of me that was being drained, rather than the physical energy part of me I had assumed was being tired out. It is the part of me that cares about everyone else that gets overwhelmed, not my physical body.

Another realisation that has changed the way I understand myself, is that there are people out there who can talk to others and listen to their stories, experiences, worries, angers, and fears without feeling them and processing them as their own. I can't do that. When people tell me their stuff, I feel it as if it was my own stuff. I can't not do it. I can't stop my mind from dwelling on it. If I am told something upsetting I will feel that upset, sometimes for days. It consumes and overwhelms me. It disables me.

So, the understanding that emotional labour disables me dawned. It's a very difficult thing to process. I cannot just stop caring for people. I am unwilling to stop connecting with people. I need connection. I crave it.

In my times of self imposed isolation as part of my self care strategy to avoid or recover from overwhelm, I always feel intensely lonely and broken.

I lament the loss of past relationships as a result of my withdrawal due to what I now recognise as emotional overwhelm, but the fact is- I simply cannot keep up with other people a lot of the time.

Ironically, I have been told I am intense. I never thought intense was bad…. but I am told I am too intense, so it has become a point of insecurity for me. If I approach new friendships without tempering myself I worry I will drown others with my friendship and remain lonely. Yet, I do not want others to withdraw from me.

Online typed communication through messaging apps has been a revelation for me. It removes the need to process conversations through spoken language and listening, and offers me opportunities for connection that I didn't have before. It protects me somewhat from overwhelm, as I can choose when I will engage and avoid it when I need to. Somehow it is more socially acceptable to have long breaks for processing between comments in online communication than in face to face. It also protects others from me. If I am too much then they can ignore me until they are ready without feeling so awkward about doing it to my face. To be clear, that was not an self depreciating statement- it is an acknowledgement that worrying about how others see me and experience me is another kind of emotional labour that I do.

As it becomes more obvious to me that some days I am quite disabled by the emotional labour I do, I have to find the strength to do the emotional labour for myself that is required to see myself that way. Admitting to yourself that some days you will forget to get dressed, eat before becoming faint, use the bathroom before it is urgent, or remember to check if there is food for your family's dinner, is not easy. Especially when you've been raised in and by a society that values action and uses it as a measure of worth. Reminding myself that I am enough, that I have value- even though disabled- is necessary, but is also emotional labour. And so I sometimes feel trapped in a cycle of overwhelm and impairment. It is not a comfortable place to be.

Realising that part of my struggles toward self acceptance is because of gender stereotypes and the fact that my disability is not and will not be

accepted by many as being legitimate is also something that forces me to do emotional labour. On my behalf and that of others. Another tiring cycle to process my way through.
The unfairness of it often feels heavy to me. I see its impacts in all corners of my life. My work life, relationships and interactions with my children.

When you consider that emotional labour is the work we do to care about others and all their preferences and needs, and that it is expected of us- particularly if we are women- but that for many Autistic people it requires significant internal resources, can't be sustained without significant energy for more than short periods of time, and is a marker of being a good friend, you probably can see why having to use energy for emotional labour impacts on executive function.

When something that is work for me, and debilitating work at times, is seen by others as something I should do without question, there is a real problem.

The problem is not that I don't care (something I have been accused of in the past), it is that I do care and the cost to me is enormous, impacting not only on my thoughts and feelings but my ability to physically get things done as well.

inertia

I've been writing this book for a while. A couple of years actually. At the time of sitting to write this chapter I have a deadline three weeks from now by which I hope to have the entire book finished. I haven't been writing the chapters in order, but rather as my brain will allow me to access the thought processes I need for each topic. As I sit to write about inertia I have only three chapters to go before the book is complete. I was talking to a friend about this three book project just last night, and as we were talking about the process of writing I commented on my frustration that I only have three chapters to go but that I seem to be "stuck on inertia". As I acknowledged the irony my friend laughed and laughed. Adding to that sense of irony was that the other two chapters I'm struggling to complete are about assertiveness and courage. I joined in the laughter, and internally hoped that the conversation was enough to get me unstuck.

My understanding of the broad concept of inertia, as used generally in society and not in science, was that it was a state of moving slowly and steadily in one direction, or being sluggish or engaging in minimal activity. I don't know if I misunderstood how people were using it, but since I began to look into the idea of "Autistic inertia" my understanding of the word has definitely changed.

My understanding of autistic inertia is closer to the definition used in physics: "the properties of matter by which it retains its state of rest or its velocity along a straight line so long as it is not acted upon by an external force".

For me personally when I say I'm experiencing a state of inertia I'm identifying that in someway I feel stuck, but it's not necessarily that I'm not doing anything. There are certainly times when I experience overwhelming exhaustion and so I need to rest, or be in active, for a period of time, but I don't refer to that as inertia, I refer to that as rest.

I experienced two different kinds of inertia state. A high activity inertia, and a low activity inertia. In both of these states I am doing, I am productive, I am active. And in both of the states it seems to take an external influence to change the state I am in. It probably sounds fairly unremarkable that I would identify these two states – high activity and low activity – but it is the adding of the inertia that is what causes me a challenge.

If I am in a state of low activity inertia and I can't interrupt it without an external influence, the challenge is that I may need or want to be achieving more in order to meet a deadline want to avoid some other constraint consequence, but be able to. This state of low activity inertia has been responsible for a great deal of discomfort in my life.

If I'm in a state of high activity inertia and I can't interrupt it without an external influence, the challenge is that I may need or want to be pacing myself or resting in order to avoid exhaustion and burn out, but be unable to. The state of high activity inertia has been responsible from many periods of essential and unavoidable rest in order to recover from having done too much.

The frustrating thing I experience with inertia is that I can know there is a better way to regulate my energy expenditure and my personal resources, and still not have capacity to change what I'm doing. And the inertia states can last for weeks, sometimes even months.

For me managing inertia is made a lot easier if I maintain a system of inflexible routines in my week. I use alarms to remind myself of my routines. There are key points in my day which reminders are set by my wise self in advance. In a way I am my own external interruption that breaks my inertia. There is an alarm for waking up and an alarm for getting up. There is an alarm for taking a lunch break. If I begin a task that I know is likely to induce an inertia state I will set an alarm to remind me to finish for the day so that I don't skip the important tasks of eating and taking care of my hygiene and getting into bed at a reasonable hour. I am most likely to slip into an inertia state if I achieve a feeling of flow during an activity that I enjoy, so the alarms I sent intended to interrupt me at the beginning of an activity are incredibly important. And annoying. I do not enjoy the setting of alarms or being interrupted by them, but I learned "the hard way" that failing to use them sets me up to fail to meet my own self care needs.

rigidity

"Rigid"

"Inflexible"

"Restricted and repetitive behaviours"

Accusations often levelled at autistic people.

Let's go straight to the source. The diagnostic criteria for autism as stated in the Diagnostic and Statistical manual of Mental Disorders, Fifth Edition.

{.....first I'll pause to acknowledge that autism isn't a mental disorder.....}

Here is the section in the DSM diagnostic criteria for Autism that asks diagnosticians to assess rigid, inflexible, restricted and repetitive behaviour:

>> Criteria B

Restricted, repetitive patterns of behavior, interests, or activities, as manifested by at least two of the following, currently or by history (examples are illustrative, not exhaustive; see text):

1. Stereotyped or repetitive motor movements, use of objects, or speech (e.g.,simple motor stereotypies, lining up toys or flipping objects, echolalia, idiosyncratic phrases).
2. Insistence on sameness, inflexible adherence to routines, or ritualized patterns of verbal or nonverbal behavior (e.g., extreme distress at small changes, difficulties with transitions, rigid thinking patterns, greeting rituals, need to take same route or eat same food every day).
3. Highly restricted, fixated interests that are abnormal in intensity or focus (e.g., strong attachment to or preoccupation with unusual objects, excessively circumscribed or perseverative interests).
4. Hyper- or hypo- reactivity to sensory input or unusual interest in sensory aspects of the environment (e.g., apparent indifference to pain/temperature, adverse response to specific sounds or textures,

excessive smelling or touching of objects, visual fascination with lights or movement).

Now, before I go through and explain my thoughts on the statements included in the DSM and quoted above, I'd like to first point out that all human brains- regardless of neurotype- prefer to conserve energy, take shortcuts, make predictions (whether they are proven correct or not) and operate reactively and defensively to those predictions, and have countless cognitive biases at play at any given time that contribute to less than ideal behavioural strategies intended to meet needs.

The DSM does a great job at noting behaviour that indicates distress as a result of unmet needs. It also pathologises those behaviours and leaves it open for medical practitioners to indiscriminately consider them maladaptive and dysfunctional.

As an autistic person, who has been proven to meet the diagnostic criteria, I can see through my own experience how some of the behaviours noted in the DSM can definitely cause problems for autistic people by limiting opportunities in both experience and personal growth. And simultaneously I object to both the wording in the

DSM and the way the information is used to pathologise and criticise autistic people.

The rigidity and inflexibility observed by others in autistic people is a valid coping strategy used by them to cope with overwhelm and manage unmet need where there is insufficient to support from others to do so. These are not random behaviours that occur for no reason or in isolation, and they do not need to be treated, fixed, or cured. They serve a purpose and they are useful to the autistic person.

Let's take point 2 as an example for discussion. "Insistence on sameness, inflexible adherence to routines, or ritualised patterns of verbal or non-verbal behaviour". It is precisely the strategies carried out in the form of micro routines, shortcuts in communication, methods of knowing what to expect in my day, predictability of sensory input, and reducing the impact of other people's changeability, that make my day manageable and give me the capacity to care for myself, my family, and to do my job in ways that allow me to be flexible with my clients when they need me to. If I wasn't rigid and inflexible, using restricted and repetitive behaviours, I would not be able to self care, raise my children in healthy ways, maintain friendships and interact socially, and run two businesses that support many people in my local community and further.

I could speak in detail to the other three points as well, and it would be along the same lines. In brief: Stereotyped or repetitive motor movements, or stimming, helps me stay calm when I'm under duress. My so called fixated interests that others consider abnormal in intensity provide me opportunity to exercise my mind, calm my body, and soothe my nervous system while being an opportunity for creativity and inventiveness. Addressing the idea of reactivity to sensory input takes a little more nuance because my actual emotional indifference to pain has caused me harm, however it is still not pathological, and on the flip side of that coin is an incredibly beautiful experience of the world that holds me in awe of our environment and helps me appreciate so many things about the world around me.

Autism is not a set of behaviours. It is a neurotype. People with an autistic neurotype can certainly be said to behave in certain ways. Some of those are stereotyped and inaccurate, some of them are stereotyped and accurate, some of them are little known or acknowledged. Most of them are not properly understood.

Rigidity is a tool. Any tool over used or applied in inappropriate circumstances can cause problems. Before we decide across the board that rigidity in autistic people is bad, let's use curiosity and try to understand what the purpose of the rigidity is, what valid use does it have in the current situation, what need is it meeting? If the rigidity is actually contextually unhelpful, the best way to support the person is to help resolve the underlying unmet need. And insistence that the behaviour change without meeting needs first is very likely to result in increased rigidity.

For myself I have learnt the crucial importance of responding to my observations I was unusual rigidity in myself with graciousness and gentleness, and with curiosity about what my needs are. This has completely changed my life for the better.

independent

Do you live independently? I do. Or so I'm told.

I have six children, some who are now adults, and some who still rely heavily on me for support. I run an advocacy and education business. I buy food, pay bills, and drive my car. I make and go to appointments, deal with necessary bureaucracy, and I vote.

By societies definition I am independent.

Except I'm not.

I rely on the support of other people for a great many things.

When I am having difficulty with a decision I have people I can talk to and that helps me clarify my thoughts. I offer the same listening ear to others. When I am overwhelmed with something I have people I can turn to for support. I do the same for them if they need it. I have friends who I share with and receive emotional support from. I support them too. In my local community, we support each other and help each other however we can. In the international community I am part of I have friends I value and who value me. We share opinions, information, advocacy, and laughs.

I have a best friend and romantic partner in my life. He offers a listening ear, is a sounding board, provides practical help and feedback, challenges me to do and be better, loving me on my best days and loving me the same when I am at my worst and struggling the most. I offer the same to him. We are individuals with our own strengths and challenges and together we aim to offer each other a balance of connection and independence that works for us.

I also receive help and support from my children. They contribute to the running fo our household. The older children watch over the younger children sometimes. They ask me if I am okay if they notice I seem down. They add humour and joy to the day.

Admittedly, on a day when I am tired and "over it" I may be guilty of muttering to myself over the kitchen sink 'why am I the only one who cleans up around here?', but that is frustration, not fact. The same goes when one of the children says 'you never help me'. They know it's not true. We try to be gracious about frustrated outbursts, as another way of supporting each other.

The truth is, in our house we share the load. We make mess together. We clean up together. We learn together. We make mistakes (sometimes together). We work together. We play together. I don't expect anyone in my family to do all the things on their own, and they don't expect me to either. We all contribute what we can when, we can. We all have value here.

All the relationships I am part of involve giving and taking.
We are connected in some ways and we are independent in some ways.

We are interdependent.

interdependent

The prefix inter- means 'between; among: mutually; reciprocally'
The word dependent means contingent on or determined by: requiring someone or something for financial, emotional, or other support: unable to do without:
Interdependent: (of two or more people or things) dependent on each other

Yes, interdependent describes my family well. I suspect it describes a lot of families. In fact, I'd go as far as to say it describes our society well. We each offer something different. Some of us grow food, some of us treat illness, some of us teach others, some of us remove waste, some of us provide clothing, some housing, some tools, some toys. Some of us are storytellers, some of us are artists, some are supporters, some are enforcers, some are protectors. All these things add value to our society. The things we do impact on other people, and their actions impact us. We work together to provide services to each other, and we show trust in each other when we do things like drive our cars, leave our children in schools, and eat food made for us by others.

We are interdependent.

Unfortunately we are also competitive. Many of us think that doing (and doing more, bigger, better, and for more money) is the only way to add value. I don't think that is true. I think we all add value just by being. Just the same as in my family, our society works on the basis that we all contribute what we can, when we can. We all have value and we all add value.

There are times when a member (could be any one) of my family has nothing to give but their presence. There are times when I have nothing to offer than just being here. There are people in our society who are the same. Sometimes there is a reason they can't do for a short while, sometimes they can't do for a long while. Sometimes some of us can only offer that we are here. There is nothing wrong with that. It all still works. The contribution of being is just as valuable as the contribution of doing. We need all of us here. We need the diversity that naturally occurs in humanity to make us what we are. We all have value. We are interdependent.

It took me a long time to start to become comfortable with not being independent. It's such a strong message that comes from society. But it has been crucial in learning to live well as an Autistic person who needs different, and sometimes more, support than others do in some situations. If I bought into the idea, as many do, that I have something to prove and that I have to do it all on my own and be independent, my life would be a complete shambles. I am autistic! I need help to live well. I need more help than many of the people I know. And that is okay.

Now, I'm not saying that it never stings a bit that I need so much support. It does. There is some internalised ableism in me that whispers into my thoughts that I should be able to do better. I am not saying that I never have moments when I feel like I need them more than they need me. I do feel that way. But I am learning to rationalise instead of catastrophise. I remind myself to keep asking for the help I need to live well. I remind myself, none of us are truly independent, and my needs are as valid as anybody else, even when they are different or more.

I am also not saying that there is a complete imbalance in the relationships in my life. The key to all the support I receive, and what makes it healthy, is that all the people who support me respect my autonomy and privacy.

They listen to me when I say what I need and they provide that without questioning the validity of my request. And they don't get in my space when I haven't requested them to be there. They don't tell me I am wrong about myself.

They give me the privacy I need to rest and recover when that is necessary. They live their own lives, apart from me. Even the guy in my life. Privacy and autonomy is important for all people. Retaining our individuality is essential to maintaining healthy relationships.

And because the relationships I receive support within are respectful and healthy, they not only support me but also give me the opportunity offer support. I have as much to give as I receive, in different ways maybe, but it isn't one way street! I receive from them and I give into them. We all give and take. These relationships are interdependent. Everybody benefits.

I firmly believe that independence is a myth, and should be removed from the goals put onto disabled people. Instead we should be teaching everyone, regardless of our ability or disability, how to live in interdependence. How to recognise our own challenges and strengths. How to ask for the help we need without shame. How to offer into relationships for the benefit of others. There is not one person who has nothing to offer! We all benefit from healthy interdependent relationships that are respectful and honour autonomy and privacy.

pendulum

I find myself in an uncomfortable state of shifting thoughts and feelings sometimes. I am continually learning to live better with an increased understanding of my needs. But writing about it is easier than the doing of it. It is one thing to process these things as thoughts, and another entirely to live it.

Sometimes I know that understanding myself leads to an increased ability to accept who I am, to look after my needs more effectively, cope better with stressors, and move through life more gently. I know it in my head. And I feel it in my heart when I do things differently than I used to.

There is less anxiety and exhaustion when I allow myself to slow when I am overwhelmed instead of pushing against it like I am trying to break through a chain link fence with my bare hands.

There is less overwhelm when I am brave enough to say no to things I know will cause stress that I should avoid.

There is less stress when I acknowledge my sensory needs and am not ashamed to own that they are real and not unreasonable.

Sometimes my mind slips back into the habit of playing the old record that tells me I am not good enough.

"You should be able to do this."
"You used to do it all the time…."
"It's not that hard. Just push through."
"If you try harder…."
"They can do it."
"Why can't you just….?"
"You aren't contributing as much as them."
"You could be more….."
"You are so disorganised…."
"…. messy ….."
"…. …. unreliable …."
"It's no wonder people don't want to be around you."

And it goes on, round and round, over and over.

I can try to ignore it while I muse about the ableism ingrained in my thought processes. But when I am completely honest, I have to admit that sometimes I do want to be able to do lots of things that others do. The pull of normality- what ever that is- is there. I know that it is not reality that being not me would resolve any of this angst, but sometimes I wish for it. Sometimes I do long for ease.

Sometimes I just can't manage to feel like enough. I want to, rather than just postulating that I am, and feeling like a hypocrite for not being able to truly believe it of myself, even though it's what I tell others with honesty that I believe about them. But sometimes, I just can't.

I can engage in positive self talk. Reminding myself that I **am** good enough. That my value is **not** tied up in what I do, or don't, or try. But theorising is different than being sure. And I want to be sure, deep down in the core of me. And I worry that it's been too much of my life that I didn't know myself and now it is too late. I fear that I won't change these old habits and this will be a battle I will fight until I have no fight left.

Sometimes I give in to the fear and let myself slip back into doing things the way I think others expect me to. And I am reminded of how much that just doesn't work out well for me. I end up in a mess, needing to take days at a time of not doing anything while my body and mind process the accumulation of too much input. Too much noise. Too much listening. Too much seeing. Too much doing. Too much feeling. Too much being. Too much remembering. Too much processing. Just too much. Sometimes I need the reminder that self care is essential.

Sometimes I make a good choice. Sometimes I manage a few good choices in a row. I achieve goals, I can see milestones. It feels good. I feel empowered. I can see how persisting with this self development, with breaking habits and leaning in to my unfolding understanding of who I am and how I work, is making me a better person.

And so I shift and swing. I am tired though, of this pendulum. I have been impatient for when the times of clarity and confidence are more frequent than the times of worry, fear, and feelings of inadequacy. And over years they are increasing.

But sometimes it still feels like not enough, and I wonder how I can make it all shift faster so that I can move away from this unease inside about who I am going to turn out to be. I know who I've tried to be. I know who I don't want to be. I don't know where I will end up though. It is unsettling, this stage of not knowing. Logically, I know that I will change forever, until I die, and that is also an uncomfortable thought.

Often a large part of me wants to just settle on something and stop there to rest in predictability. But that would mean a halt in progress as well.

I am trying to rest instead in the knowledge that self acceptance is a process, and that the swinging is to be expected. I am trying to be mindful of the fact that a pendulum serves a purpose. It has a valuable job, working to help keep things ticking along. Each swing serves a purpose and measures a moment in time. That is not unpredictable in the bigger picture. Rather it is deliberate and purposeful. Recognising that this stage is part of the process that I can rely on to move me toward self acceptance is reassuring, and gives me confidence to acknowledge the discomfort and keep riding out the shifts and swings.

labels

"Labels are for cans, not for people".
But why?

I have no problem with labelling and don't see it as a negative thing. I see labels simply as words used to describe. So for me these would include woman, mother, friend, daughter, sister, untidy, advocate, forgetful, teacher, anxious, writer, autistic, fair skinned, clumsy, gardener, etc. These are factual descriptors, neither "good" nor "bad".

I decided to look up the word label, to prove my point that there is nothing negative about labels. I was surprised to find this,
Label, *noun: a classifying phrase or name applied to a person or thing, especially one that is inaccurate or restrictive*
Label, *verb: assign to a category, especially inaccurately or restrictively*

How did I miss this? How did I not know that I am supposed to see labels as negative?
I asked some friends what they think, and they said they don't see labels as negative either (unless someone else is applying them to a person who didn't ask them to, but that's another conversation). I began to wonder if the word label has always been seen as negative, and I had just not picked up on it.

I brought the old 1995 printed book dictionary down off the book shelf and looked it up the old fashioned way. I found this,
Label: *a short word or phrase of description for a person, group, movement, etc.*

There is absolutely nothing there about it being negative, inaccurate or restrictive…. so something changed in the last 20 years. I suspect what has changed is the public conversation around disability.

The spaces I see conversations around labels being negative are largely groups of parents of disabled children. "I don't like labels" they say. "My child is not defined by their disability".

Define: *state or describe exactly the nature, scope, or meaning of• give the meaning of (a word or phrase), especially in a dictionary. • make up or establish the character or essence of*

I just don't see how having an accurate descriptor of a person- who they are and what they need to get the most out of life- is a bad thing. Isn't that just helpful information?

There seem to be things that it is acceptable to be defined by or labelled as. "Attractive", "Happy", "Clever", "Healthy". And some things that are not acceptable to be defined by or labelled as. "Fat", "Grumpy", "Disabled".

We are told we should be ashamed of and try to change the things about ourselves that others deem to be inherently "bad". "Don't label yourself". "I'm sorry you are ____, but," they say with a hopeful lilt to their voices, "you don't have to let it define you."

Why?

Why is it bad to be labelled by something that explains who you are? Why is it negative to be defined by something that contributes to making you who you are?

The fact is, I actually like my labels. I am happy for them to define me. They are factual descriptors that give information. When I share them with you I do it with pride in who I am, what I have experienced and how those things shaped me. And I share with you in the hope it will help us both for you to understand me. Not because I want you to feel sorry for me or reassure me.

It's an interesting dynamic really, noticing which things are considered acceptable to have define us and which aren't.

Autism defines me.

There are other things that define me too- gender, my appearance, marital status, being a parent, my chosen work, how I spend time and who I spend it with…. It's not bad to be defined by things, whether you chose to have them as part of your life or not.

We are also told that children don't place as much value in labels as adults do, so we must be careful not to put things on them. This is not true. I have yet to meet a child who would not be upset by a negatively perceived label given them or proud of a positively perceived one. Neurodivergent, disabled, or not. Part of the problem is that we teach our children that some labels are negative when they are not and should never be treated as they are.

I was an autistic child, even though unidentified. I understood labels then and I still do now. I'm still living with the impacts of some of the things I was labelled. "Naughty". "Rude". "Lazy". I much prefer my Autistic label than any of those.

The more I journey through claiming my identity, the more I'd love to see "label" return to being a value neutral word, one used simply to convey the idea that we are passing on information to each other that is helpful in our efforts to understand what we each are and need.

paradox

It might seem to contradict what I have said in other places,
It even feels a bit incongruous to me to say it,
because so much of my life is about being Autistic and identifying as Autistic,
and unpacking all that means,
including all the parts of me that work in Autistic ways;
But autism is not the reason why I do everything that I do.

I do not make all my choices the way I do only because I am Autistic.
I do not enjoy all the things I enjoy simply because I am Autistic,
I do not dislike all the things I dislike just because I am Autistic.
Being Autistic helps to make me who I am,
but so do my personality, my experiences,
and the cumulative effect of the decisions I have made throughout my life.

I am a writer,
an advocate,
an activist;
I am a critical thinker,
a non-conformist,
a dissident.

I am a mentor,
a teacher,
a student;
I am a parent,
a daughter, sibling,
a friend, and colleague.

I am happy, sad,
joyful, angry,
intentional, and disorganised;
I am confident, insecure,
decisive, hesitant,
brave, and terrified.

Like all people I am a paradox,
a complex and beautiful mess of contradictions
and truths, a balancing of harmony and discord;
Simultaneously content and dissatisfied,
striving for more while wishing for less,
creating chaos and craving calm.

Being Autistic is a part of all of that, but I am not just Autistic.

strong

Sometimes people tell me that I am the only Autistic adult they know. I tell them that I think they do know others, but those people haven't disclosed to them, preferring to do their best to blend in as much as they can.

A tricky thing about being Autistic is that we are socialised to think it means we are so completely different that it's going to be totally obvious. But in reality, there is nothing we experience or do as Autistic people that is outside what the normal experience of being human includes. It's just that we experience things with more intensity and at higher frequency, and this influences our behaviour. For some of us this means we are easily noticed by others as being different. For some of us this is not the case, and we "hide in plain sight".

The world we live in now is incredibly difficult for Autistic people because it has become so full on in sensory and social ways, and in order to blend in we have to push ourselves past what we can easily cope with to be included. Even the DSM, which is not an ideal tool in many ways, acknowledges that autism goes unidentified until a persons capacity to cope (ie mask) is exhausted.

So, when we begin our process of self discovery it's really difficult to not have to go through thinking that maybe we are just making it all up because we aren't that different than everyone else! And we aren't. Until we look deeper. And that's what has to happen.

People who become confident to self identify as Autistic, or to make themselves vulnerable to the medical, pathologising diagnostic assessment process, are remarkably resilient in that we have come to a point of self understanding that is uncommon in humans, and are willing to talk about it. It's like learning to see yourself in full colour instead of just black and white. Once you see the detail, the shades, the tones, the highlights, the nuances, you understand so much better, and you want to share that understanding with others.

The Autistic community is amazing in many ways, but it's this that continually astounds me- we are are some of the strongest, most self aware, and most resilient people. We often apply our strength to doing what it takes to keep others around us happy instead of looking after our own needs though, and we are also some of the most self critical and self deprecating, simply because we've been socialised to doubt ourselves for being different. Which is ironic both because we are different, and we aren't. It's a really tough place to be, socially and internally. But we are strong.

functioning

We've all heard someone called "high functioning" or "low functioning". To illustrate why these terms are really problematic, I'm going to tell you some things about myself.

I am a person who
- has difficulty adjusting to change
- experiences an unpredictable combination of situational mutism and/or difficulty reading and writing when overwhelmed or stressed
- relies on familiarity and routine
- has poor sleep quality and difficulty falling asleep
- experiences significant sensory challenges
- experiences sensory discomfort that interferes with self care tasks
- has a restricted diet due to sensory preferences
- needs help to use public transport
- finds it hard to start tasks
- finds it difficult to switch tasks
- is confused by colloquialisms

- goes through periods of intense focus on tasks or interests that interrupt regular activities and cause self neglect
- forgets to eat and use the bathroom until it is quite urgent
- needs help and support to work more than one day a week
- has a lot of anxiety
- fidgets and stims

I am also a person who
- has two university degrees: one in teaching and one in psychology
- is a self employed mentor, advocate, and trainer
- maintains my own website of articles and resources
- is internationally known as a writer and resource developer, with work translated into 5 languages
- has edited two books on autism neurodiversity and parenting
- has authored a book about understanding myself as Autistic
- travelled to Geneva to make a presentation to the United Nations Committee on the Rights of Persons with Disability about the practice of seclusion and restraint in Australian schools

- worked with grassroots group to make submission to UN and supported 56 families through the process
- is on the board of two not for-profit organisations working on inclusion
- carries out advocacy at systemic and community levels, and for individuals
- provides training to teachers on how to support neurodivergent students
- runs workshops and speaks at conferences on a variety of topics
- has 6 neurodivergent children

If I didn't tell you both of these lists were my own traits, would you have assumed these were two completely different people? Many people reading this would have, and they would have thought that the first person was more low functioning than the second. In fact, many people would read the second list and think that person wasn't autistic or disabled.

When someone assumes from looking at you or reading a list of your accomplishments that you are not disabled a problem is created, because they are then not open to the possibility that you may need support.

When someone assumes from looking at you or reading a list of your challenges that you are disabled, they will often also presume that you are not competent in a lot of ways. See the problem?

"High functioning autism" is a myth. When someone refers to high functioning autism they generally mean that the autistic person doesn't seem that different than they expect a non autistic person to be, and that their autistic traits aren't noticeable enough to make the non autistic person uncomfortable. Similarly, "low functioning" or "severe" autism is often used to refer to a person whose needs are seen as inconvenient by others.

Now, I know that sometimes people use terminology they've found in the DSM - level 1, level 2 and level 3. This is based on a misinterpretation of what the DSM says. When the DSM refers to levels, it is talking about level of support needed to live well, not severity of autism.

Another thing worth noting is that often the things that get an autistic person labelled as "low functioning" are things that often co-occur alongside autism, like sleep disturbances, apraxia (that's being "non-verbal"), or dyspraxia (that's trouble with motor planning and execution, and can impact acquisition of skills including things like toileting and other self care tasks), or things like cerebral palsy, epilepsy, disordered eating and mood based disabilities. Those things are all based in neurodivergence, but they are not autism.

High and low functioning autism are not real. Autism is autism.

There is nothing high functioning about me on days when I have to spend most of my time in bed, under a weighted blanket with noise cancelling headphones on and not speaking, regardless of how I appear to you on a day when I stand before you and do my job after having prepared carefully and budgeted my energy for weeks in order to ensure I am able to do it.

If you cherry pick parts of my life and bundle them together you could put me in either box. Labelling an autistic person high or low functioning denies that, just like any other person, autistic people are complex and nuanced and subject to the full range of variations in energy and capability at any given moment in time.

uninspirational

Identity is an interesting thing. We recognise so many identity markers in our lives. And there are many that apply to me. I am called mum by six people. There is a group of lovely young people who call me aunty, their parents call me sister. I am daughter to two wonderful parents. Some people call me sensei. Some call me their mentor. I am sometimes a student, sometimes an educator or trainer. I am a friend. I've been called funny once or twice. I've been called rude more than twice, which may have been true in that moment, or it may have been an accusation because a truth spoken left someone feeling uncomfortable. I've been called disorganised, which was true, and which made me uncomfortable, so I've worked to change it with varying levels of success in different situations.

I've also been called inspirational, which made me incredibly uncomfortable, because it is not true and that will never change.

The way we tend to use "inspirational" when we refer to disabled people has connotations of "if they can do it, what's your excuse?", and "look what they have to overcome, aren't you glad you aren't them?".

Before I explain why I feel so strongly about this, I first have to mention the late Stella Young. Stella was, as far as I know, the first person to speak about "inspiration porn", and to explain in words that made so much sense to me, why calling disabled people inspirational is not okay. I'd love it if you could have a look at Stella's work. The best place to do that for a quick explanation is Stella's TED Talk "I am not your inspiration, thank you very much". I'm not going quote Stella directly here, but please do look her up.

I am going to give you my own Autistic version of why I am completely Uninspirational. You see, I am just living my life. Sure, it might look different than yours, and it probably has some significant challenges in it that the majority of people don't experience. But I'm still not inspirational. Let's look at some of the challenges.

I have a lot of sensory processing challenges. I use a pretty complex set of strategies in order to make sure I don't get overwhelmed by my sensory sensitivities, and to meet my sensory needs. I plan, self care, rest, avoid some situations and seek out others. I research to find good information and resources to help me meet my needs. I have some people in my life who help me with sensory regulation too. To manage my sensory challenges I have to be self aware and vigilant in my self care, but I am not inspirational because I do this.

I have some communication challenges. When I am overwhelmed I find spoken language difficult, so I sometimes type to communicate instead of speaking. When I am in a loud environment I have some auditory processing difficulties, so I can't always follow conversations and I use lip reading to help me. I don't always understand implied meaning, so I sometimes misunderstand words and situations and it can cause confusion. Sometimes when I ask the questions to get the information I need to understand, it can be frustrating for others and for me. To manage my communication challenges I have to be resourceful, but I am not inspirational because I do this.

I have many executive function challenges. They impact my organisation skills, my ability to stay focussed on a task, my ability to switch between tasks, my capacity to ignore distracting sensory input, and more. In order to live well, I have to be careful not to allow myself to become too tired because that is when my executive function challenges become very noticeable. I need a fair bit of routine in my life so things are predictable, and I need to constantly monitor my progress on tasks carefully to make sure I am on the right track. Sometimes I am a total mess! But sometimes I get it right. This takes persistence and resilience, but I am not inspirational because I do it.

I have self regulation challenges. Like many autistic people, I don't always read my body's internal cues well, and I experience very big emotional reactions to things that happen internally and externally. Combined with my sensory processing challenges, this is probably one of the more disabling aspects of being Autistic for me. I don't sleep very well, I forget to eat, I get overwhelmed by noise, light, and touch. When I am in pain I often don't realise it and so don't look after my body in the best ways. I experience inertia- both high activity and low activity states, that continue until I am forcibly interrupted in some way. Too long in either state of inertia is problematic. I easily overdo it and make myself very, very tired. Looking after my body takes deliberate strategising, careful planning, and the development and maintenance of healthy connections with other people who understand and can support me when I need help (even though I am sometimes too proud and reluctant to ask for help). I am not inspirational for looking after my own self regulation needs, or for asking for help when I need it.

I am simply living my life, navigating the challenges I experience as best I can on a daily basis, just like everybody else.

Some days that looks like writing articles to share with others about my experience. That makes me a thinker, a writer, an advocate, and sometimes vulnerable. But it does not make me inspirational because I do it while Autistic.

Some days living my life looks like spending time supporting my children, who are also neurodivergent, with their needs. This makes me a parent, hopefully a caring one, but I am not inspirational for doing that while Autistic.

Some days living my life looks like teaching a whole day workshop, or getting on a plane to go and speak at a conference. To do this work I need to be capable of being articulate enough to communicate ideas to others when I plan well enough, but it does not make me inspirational because I do that while Autistic.

Some days living my life looks like making beds, doing laundry, washing dishes and vacuuming floors. I might do my house work with sunglasses and noise cancelling headphones on, and definitely do it autistically, but I am still not inspirational for having a clean house while disabled.

Somedays living my life looks like weighted blankets, tears, stimming, rest and recovery, and hanging in there until the overwhelm passes so I can try again tomorrow. And I am still not inspirational. Even when I make myself vulnerable and share it for others to see.

I particularly dislike being held up as an inspirational role model to other Autistic people. This very much falls into the "if they can do it, what's your excuse" category, even though a lot of inspiration porn is aimed at non-disabled people to challenge them to do better. When I am held up to other Autistic people as someone to aspire to be like, I feel a horrible sense of competition is thrown onto us. I absolutely never approach mentoring with this mentality.

Autistic people don't need to be inspired. We need connection. Autistic peer to peer, we understand each other, empathise with each other, connect with each other. We offer stories as ways of showing solidarity and sharing ideas to try. I just don't see any Autistic community discussions that look like "if I can do it with all my autisticness so can you". What I do see is "I understand your struggle with that, here is something I tried, in case you want to try it too". That is how I approach mentoring and advocacy.

When I see other people hold me up as an example of how "successful" an Autistic person can be, because I can manage to talk about this sort of thing publicly, it makes me cringe hard. I worry that the comparison further reinforces the internal shame that the other Autistic person is probably feeling. I share my messiness and my vulnerability precisely so that other Autistic people know I don't have it all together all the time, and that I do struggle still, daily, even while doing what I do to live well. I share it because it is messy, raw, tedious, and uninspirational. It is Autistic life and we need to acknowledge all of it. I do not share it so that I can be held up as some sort of yardstick.

The thing is, every single person experiences challenges. Life is not a challenge competition in which we all should compare who has it "better" or "worse", "harder" or "easier". And even if we did, it would be impossible to measure. Some days a non autistic life is probably more difficult to navigate than my autistic life! Who decides which days those are, and whose standard do we use to measure? Saying I am inspirational because I am alive and Autistic and doing stuff is a bit of a nonsense because this is my normal and I am just doing what I do exactly like everybody else who is living their normal, Autistic and not. Each Autistic persons life has it's own unique set of challenges and triumphs that are as many and varied as the wonderfully complex members of the Autistic community. How do we decide who is having the harder day? And why should we? Can't we just acknowledge and honour each persons individual experience without comparing?

I am a lot of things, just like many other mothers, sister, friends, teachers and everybody else that I know…

I am resourceful, persistent, vigilant, self aware, resilient.

I can be organised, a good communicator, articulate, tidy, strategic, vulnerable.

I try to be caring and kind, and to have compassion for others.

I try to influence others to think differently about autism, neurodivergence and disability, and not just accept the mainstream discourse that surrounds them.

If you want to give me a compliment, use one of those words that actually talks about who I am and acknowledges what I try to do. But please, don't call me inspirational.

noncompliant

I am convinced that "noncompliant" is a mood. It is a mood I experience frequently.

I'm trying to continue to learn to break past habits of keeping those around me happy, and to allow myself to see my own value and take care of my own needs as a priority. It's some of the hardest work I do, this self care. Because so much of what we learn as young people in our society is to comply and conform. Doing differently than that takes thought and effort.

I regularly see stories of police harming people. I'm thinking about how disabled and neurodivergent people get blamed for the harm that comes to us, when really the problem is people who think they should have power and control so they forget to treat others with care, respect, and dignity.

I see stories about domestic violence and bullying. Authenticity is surely something we all deserve to feel free to show, yet for some of us it endangers our wellbeing, and sometimes our lives. I'm thinking about how to resource the neurodivergent community to keep ourselves safe without having to hide our true selves.

I hear about social skills programs designed to teach autistic children to understand and fit in with non autistic children. Sometimes I am asked to endorse them. I decline, and think about the lack of programs designed to teach non autistic people how to be accepting of difference and diversity. I'm thinking of the effort neurodivergent folks go to be part of society and the complaining that happens when we ask for just one little thing... like to be listened to.

I watch service providers, "helpers", who only offer the help they think we need instead of asking us what we actually need and want. There are too many people who assume disability is the same as incapability. I'm thinking about rights, assumptions, dignity of risk, presumption of incompetence, and thoughtless perpetuation of stigma and stereotype.

I notice my own internalised ableism and how it impacts on my internal dialogue and self talk.

I'm thinking about sensory overwhelm, stimming, needing lots of rest and recovery time, but being pressured to be productive and busy.

I'm thinking about how important it is to teach our children to say "NO".
I'm thinking about the fact it is essential that we respect it when people tell us no, so that our children understand what the word means and how to use it to look after themselves.

I am thinking about how important it is that Autistic people learn to be noncompliant. For our own safety and for the safety of our children.

assertive

I don't want to talk about noncompliance without also talking about being assertive.

Far too often an autistic child will communicate their needs and, for one reason or another, the adults around them don't do a very good job of supporting the child to have their needs met. Maybe the adults didn't understand the communication, maybe they didn't think it was that important, maybe they thought they knew better. Whatever the reason, the child has tried to tell something about them self and and they have not been heard. This results in an ongoing unmet need.

Most humans, when we have ongoing unmet needs, do things the people around us find uncomfortable to draw attention to the fact that we need something. We cry, demand, blame, yell, nag, whinge, retreat, manipulate, try to get the need met another way, ….. there are a vast range of behavioural strategies we use. And I'm not just talking about children. Adults do these things too.

If our needs are not met and we feel threatened we will become aggressive. Autistic or not. It is normal human behaviour to defend ourselves when we are threatened or under duress, even when the threat is more perceived than real.

When an autistic person uses these strategies in situations seen by others as inappropriate or an over reaction, we are labelled as having "challenging behaviours". Wouldn't it be great if we could all just acknowledge these situations for what they are? The direct result of a communication breakdown that has pushed the autistic person to use extreme measures to communicate their needs.

I'm not endorsing the use of aggression. What I want to do is to talk about how we can support autistic children, and adults, to learn assertive non compliance as a self advocacy strategy to have their needs met before they feel pushed to be aggressive in their communication.

A large part of teaching assertive non compliance is accepting a child's "no" as being reasonable

and honouring their self advocacy around things that might seem small. One way we can do this is by becoming curious rather than reactive.
It is easy when we hear a child's "no" to reactively use coercion in order to achieve the outcome we desire.

It takes more skill to pause and curiously enquire as to the reason for the "no".

Asking how we can support the child to have their needs met so that they are safe to say yes is much more likely to result in a calm and pleasant experience for all than just demanding compliance. Once a child has had experiences of their "no" being respected and their needs being met they will have the basis for the skills they need in being assertive rather than aggressive. The reason for this is that the child learns that they have options.

So, how do we meet the child's needs so they can change their no to a yes? We have to take the time to understand what the need is, why it exists and what the child would like to see happen by way of meeting the need. In a society that doesn't trust children to know themselves well enough to know what they need, it can be a real challenge for many adults to trust children in this way. And in truth, many children don't have the skill of being able to notice and communicate about their needs, not because they aren't capable, but because they have learned to distrust their own body's messages as a direct result of adults not trusting them. It's a dangerous cycle that must be interrupted.

As adults it is us that needs to do the interrupting.

Breaking this cycle involves little things like listening when a child says they don't like a food, or they are full, or that something hurts. It involves refraining from coercion and manipulation to get the child to eat the food anyway, or empty their plate, or to carry on and stop crying. It is vital that we adults begin to facilitate a deep understand about, and attention to, children's internal body messages and to help children find ways of communicating about their needs in all situations.

Worth noting is that if we don't help children to do this, they grow up to be adults who don't have the skills either. So can I encourage you to re-read this chapter with in mind that the same is true for adults as for children?

If you are an adult who is recognising that you have trouble being assertive, it is possible that much of the reason is that you didn't learn as a child that your internal body cues were reliable and to be trusted. You may need to consciously relearn to trust yourself. The practice of being mindfully aware of your body acne help with this. Yoga and martial arts are great ways to begin. My own practice of karate has been life changing in increasingly self awareness and self confidence.

Key skills that I know have helped me move toward a better understanding of myself and my needs, and toward more assertive communication, are being able to take a pause so I give myself some "buffering" time and then choosing a response instead of a reaction. This is being assertive with myself by not allowing myself to use strategies that won't serve me well in the long term. Once I can be assertive with myself it is much easier to be assertive with others.

normal

What is normal for one is not normal for another.

An intense sensory experience of the world isn't all bad and doesn't always result in sensory defensiveness.

I am definitely sensory defensive in many ways-
sudden loud noises like balloon popping, droning mechanical noises, the sound of cutlery...
light touch on my skin, any touch from people I don't know well, certain squishy textures and some rough ones...
bright lights and glare...
... all those things make me cringe and I avoid them as much as possible.

But!
I love loud music with a strong beat and excellent harmonies.

I thrive with lots of hugs and firm pressure touch from people I have loving, trusting relationships with.

My eyes and fingers take great delight in the intense colours and textures of flowers, and spring is the best time of year for enjoying this.

An intense sensory experience is definitely not all bad.

An intense sensory experience is normal for Autistic people.

Executive function funkiness is an important indicator that someone needs more support, while also being an incredible gateway to creativity and inventiveness.

I experience challenges with intermittent ability to ignore environmental or cognitive distractions, having a poor capacity for short term memory, slipping into hyper focus when it's a really inconvenient time, getting stuck in thought loops or patterns that bog me down, and my struggles with emotional regulation are ongoing.

And!

The creativity that comes with reduced impulse control gives me so much satisfaction and happiness, the way I notice tiny details that others miss is incredibly useful, experiencing emotion the way I do means I have great capacity for empathy, and my tendency to think on things so deeply can lead to insights that wouldn't occur to others.

Executive function challenges are definitely not all bad.

Executive function challenges are normal for Autistic people.

Language processing differences are challenging, and are opportunities to look at communication differently, to try new strategies and find ways to to understand the world, people and relationships, and yourself.

While difficulty understanding implied meaning, auditory processing delays and misunderstandings, and situational mutism are certainly inconvenient and at times frustrating…

Also, I have a variety of options available to me in non-speech based communication methods to reduce the frustration. Communication challenges offer me opportunities, too. For example, I have learned that when I am having more frequent and intense instances of communication difficulty it is a reliable indicator that I need to rest or create some space for myself with less demands on my cognitive energy. And recognising that I sometimes use language differently than others has prompted me and those close to me to have intentional discussions about how we can relate to each other more effectively and with more care and consideration. It's a 'two way street' in which I have learned new skills and so have they, and that builds closeness and connection in relationship.

Language processing differences are definitely not all bad.

Language processing differences are normal for Autistic people.

And neurodivergence is normal for humans. Everything a neurodivergent person experiences fits within the normal range of human experience. Neurodivergent people aren't broken. There is nothing wrong with them. Neurodivergence is normal.

courageous

I have a piece of paper stuck to the door in my office at work. It has a quote on it. One of my favourites.

> Courage doesn't always roar.
> Sometimes courage is the little voice
> at the end of the day saying,
> "I will try again tomorrow"
> *Mary Anne Radmacher*

An online search on quotes about courage will reveal a seemingly endless collection of variations on a theme: courage isn't the absence of fear but the ability to act while afraid. It's true. But I like Mary Anne Radmacher's words better. They feel gentler and hint more at the complexity of courage. At least the way I experience it.

I am courageous in ways that I find acceptable and I can manage within the bounds of my comfort. I think the same is true for all of us. Sometimes we have the capacity for courage and other times we don't. The reasons behind this are too many and too complex for me to discuss in this book- it's a book on its own, and there are others much more qualified who have written. What I do want to talk about here is how I care for myself to increase the possibility I will have the capacity for courage when I need it.

Living autistically, in a society that is so intense in so many ways, requires courage. Interacting with the sensory environments we must navigate just to gather basic daily supplies. Making and maintaining relationships in a culture that expects a very specific set of competences. Accessing education and employment inside systems that are archaic and entirely unsuited to an autistic brain and nervous system. Coping with the speed, structure, and culture of the social society surrounding us. All are so overwhelming.

And fear inducing.

Remember, it is normal and healthy to experience fear in response to danger, and in anticipation of pain.

Fear is an appropriate response to many of the societal challenges autistic people face.

Courage is an appropriate response to fear.
If I couldn't find capacity for courage, I would not be able to live the life that I prefer.

So, how?

Well….. all the things I have written about in this book, and in the rest of this "Living Autistically" series.

It is knowing myself and understanding my needs.

It is prioritising meeting my needs even when it isn't glamorous, or fun, or relatable to other people.

It is learning which of the easier, default mode things I do are helping me and which need adjustment.

It is settling into the effort of trying new ways, experimenting with strategies, seeking our moral support and new ideas.

It is accepting that there are things I am just not great and and likely won't ever be, then finding work arounds or ways to outsource.

It is guarding myself wisely from bad advise, unhelpful influence, and short term feel good solutions, in favour of carefully selected trustworthy counsel and long term investment in healthy strategies.

It is figuring out the unique combination of things that work for me, and no one else, and loving myself well enough to do them. Even when I don't want to. And to keep trying again and again until I am doing what is needed. Most of the time. Enough of the time. How it feels right for me.

That is what I can find courage for consistently at this point in my life. The courage for anything else that needs it follows when I am prioritising my needs.

My courage isn't a roar. At least, very rarely. More often than not it is simply about acting in ways that care for myself, even while I am fearful and uncertain, over and over again until things work the way I need them to.

perfect

All these things I have learned about myself since I realised I am Autistic,
all the time I have spent researching and reading,
all the energy I have sunk into self reflection,
and all the time I have spent actively seeking out self understanding,
have all been for one reason.
I thought I was broken and I was trying to fix myself.

But,
I am not broken, I remind myself
I just have a brain that is wired for an intense experience of the world
And a body that reacts to that in ways considered atypical by many

I am not broken, I tell others
You just don't see things the way I do
And you behave differently than me

I..am..not..broken…. I..am..not..broken….
I..am..not..broken…. I mutter softly
Through my anxiety and fear
And I do what I need to to look after myself when I am overwhelmed

I am not broken!! I yell to the mountains
When I take myself to nature and sit in solitude
And let my stressed sensory system calm and relax

I am not broken. I force myself to say
Through hot frustrated tears
When internalised ableism gets the better of me and I don't really believe myself

I. Am. Not. Broken. I whisper fiercely
When I have to prioritise self care because I just can't do another thing
And the world feels too hard, too harsh, too demanding, and too much

I am not broken, I exclaim. Joyfully.
Recognising reflections of myself in so many others in neurodivergent community
And sharing, understanding, laughing, supporting, growing… together

I am repaired and I am whole, I sigh contentedly

Cocooned in the dark, quiet, stillness of my safe place
Knowing that being different is not wrong and that I am valuable just as I am

I am not broken, I repeat
Over and over and over and over again
Because I am not wrong
And it is right to remind myself
That success is subjective
That what works for me is for me to decide, and
That there is nothing wrong with being my authentic self

I am not broken, I remind myself
Every day in many ways
Because it is true

I am not broken

I am not a broken normal person, I am a perfectly normal autistic person.

Perfectly Normal Autistic

www.ingramcontent.com/pod-product-compliance
Lightning Source LLC
Chambersburg PA
CBHW071834290426
44109CB00017B/1818